An Illustrated Guide to the Doll as Used in Fashion

by

Max von Boehn

British Library Cataloguing-in-Publication Data
A catalogue record for this book is available from
the British Library

THE FASHION DOLL

MORE skilfully than any other nation the French utilized dolls as a profitable means of propaganda, employing them freely in the service of their trade in ladies' fashions. French fashions,

FIG. 126. "HAMPELMANN": PEASANT
GIRL IN PARTS
French engraving. About 1750

FIG. 127. "HAMPELMANN": BALLERINA
IN PARTS
French engraving. About 1750

and not by chance, are highly favoured by women of all the five continents. Yet only rarely are these fashions real inventions of Paris; usually they come from other sources; but there they are executed with so much taste, and the French women know how to wear their clothes with such a peculiar charm, that Paris fashions capture all eyes and are eagerly imitated. The French never spare themselves self-praise, and just as some-

1

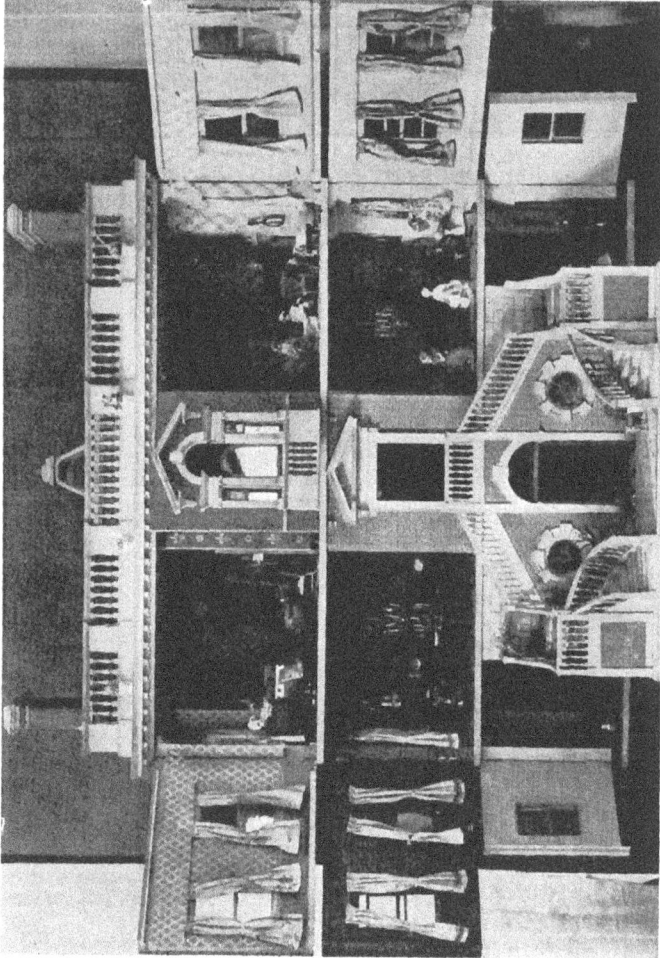

FIG. 128. ENGLISH DOLL'S HOUSE, ABOUT 1760
Lent to the Bethnal Green Museum, London, by Mrs Walter Tate
By permission of the Victoria and Albert Museum

thing always remains in the mind when we hear slander of others, so this general and constantly repeated self-praise never misses its mark, the hearer always having it impressed on his memory. At a time when as yet the press was non-existent, long before the invention of such mechanical means of reproduction as the woodcut and the copperplate, to the doll was given the

FIG. 129. THE BREAKFAST (DETAIL)
Engraving by Lépicié after the painting by Boucher. About 1740

task of popularizing French fashions abroad. The fashion doll first makes its appearance in the account books of the French Court. Queen Isabeau of Bavaria got dolls sent to the Queen of England to give that youthful monarch an idea of the fashions of the French Court. In 1396 Robert de Varennes, the Court tailor of Charles VI, received 459 francs for a doll's wardrobe executed by him. As this was a considerable sum, it is to be concluded that the dolls were life-size, made to the measure of the English Queen. The next record dates from a century later. In 1496 Anne of Brittany, the then reigning queen, ordered a great doll to be made and dressed for the Spanish Queen,

DOLLS OF THE PERIOD OF THE FRENCH EMPIRE

About 1800-10

4

Isabella the Catholic. Isabella was then forty-three years old, an age which in a period when girls were wont to marry at fourteen years seemed to be on the threshold of senility, but was very smart and particular about her dress, never giving audience to foreign ambassadors twice in the same costume. This fact

FIG. 130. CHILD WITH DOLL (NUN)
J. B. S. Chardin

must have been well enough known in the French Court; the actual dress put on this doll was deemed to be wanting in perfection, and it was decided to re-equip it with a much costlier *ensemble*.

Marie de' Medici, when Henry IV, no longer in his first youth, took her as his second wife, was full of eagerness to learn all about the prevailing French fashions. "Frontenac tells me," writes the King to her, "that you wish to have samples of our fashions: I am therefore sending you several model dolls." In the seventeenth century this export of dolls, hitherto left to

6

DOLLS AND PUPPETS

chance, was systematized and organized. Furetière in his *Roman Bourgeois* informs us that in the *salon* of Mlle de Scudéry, the well-known novelist, there used to stand two dressed dolls—the one a large *pandora* in full costume, the other a small *pandora* in *négligé*. Fashion dolls of this kind were first sent to England and then to other countries. As early as 1642 the Strasbourg

FIG. 131. GERMAN DOLL
Stuffed body with a china head (1850–60), dress, and *coiffure* (1878).
Height, 68 cm.
Germanisches National-Museum, Nürnberg

satirist Moscherosch ridiculed the German women of his time for getting dolls sent to them from Paris in order that they might copy costume and *coiffure*. Still more sharp expressions appeared in the anonymous lampoon of 1689 called *Der deutsch-französische Modegeist* (*The Spirit of Franco-German Fashion*). "And the worst of it is," we read there, "that not only do our women-folk themselves travel to France, but they pay as many thalers for their models, these dressed-up dolls, to be sent to them, as would serve them to emulate the very frippery of the devil." Such satire, however, did not trouble the German ladies. A certain A. Leo, who from 1671 to 1673 accompanied a Herr von Lüttichau on the Grand Tour, in

7

THE FASHION DOLL

1673 sent from Paris to his pupil's aunt, Frau von Schleinitz, a doll "which he had got made in the latest fashion, especially in so far as the head and hair were concerned."

FIG. 132. WAX DOLL: TOWN LADY, MUNICH, 1877
Spielzeug-Museum, Sonneberg

The fashion doll penetrated as far as Venice. At the Sensa, the fourteen-day fair in the Piazza S. Marco, was annually exhibited a doll clad in the latest Parisian fashion, and for a whole twelve months this remained the dressmakers' model.

The chief destination for these exported fashion dolls was England, and even war could not hinder their passage. Writing in 1704, the Abbé Prévost observes:

By an act of gallantry which is worthy of being noted in the chronicles of history for the benefit of the ladies the ministers of both Courts granted a special pass to the mannequin; that pass was

FIG. 133. THE CHEVALIER DE PANGE
Painting by Drouais. About 1760

always respected, and during the times of greatest enmity experienced on both sides the mannequin was the one object which remained unmolested.

Such announcements appeared in the English papers as "Last Saturday the French doll for the year 1712 arrived at my house in King Street, Covent Garden." During the Regency the French Ambassador in London was Dubois, who later became Cardinal, and, in order to win favour with the English ladies, he wrote to the dressmaker Mlle Fillon in Paris, ordering her to send a large mannequin designed to show how the French women were dressed and coiffeured and how they wore their underclothing. His nephew, however, in reply to his order stated that this was not such a simple matter, that it would cost at least 300 francs, and that neither Mme Law nor Mlle Fillon

9

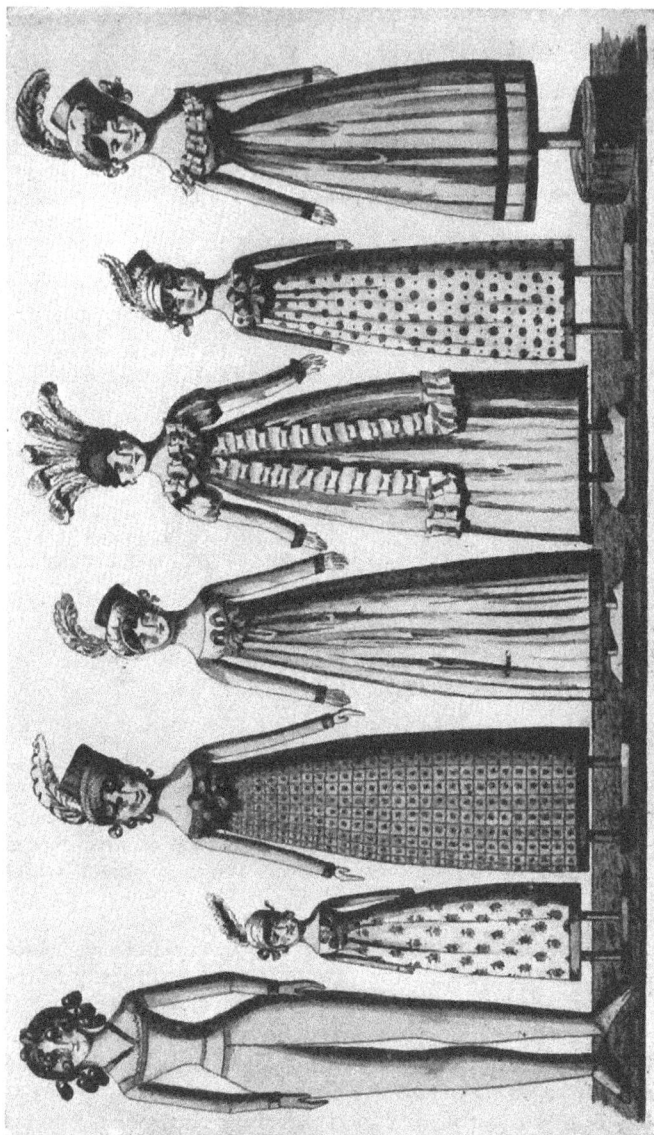

FIG. 134. DOLLS FROM THE PERIOD OF THE FRENCH EMPIRE
About 1800–10
From *Histoire des Jouets*, by Henri d'Allemagne

10

would risk the expense unless they were sure of being reimbursed. In 1727 Lady Lansdowne sent to Queen Caroline's ladies-in-waiting a mannequin in Court dress with the request that, after

FIG. 135. BRIDE (NÜRNBERG), MIDDLE OF THE NINETEENTH CENTURY
Bayerisches National-Museum, Munich. Photo Kester and Co.

it had circulated among them, they should dispatch it to Mrs Tempest the dressmaker.

In his trade lexicon of 1723 Savary mentions the beautiful dolls, elaborately coiffeured and richly dressed, which were sent to foreign Courts. No longer were they called, as formerly,

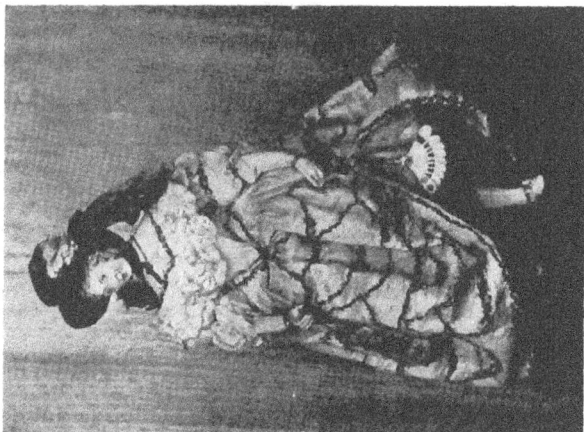

12

by the name of *pandoras*, being styled now 'dolls of the **Rue Saint-Honoré**,' a street which in the eighteenth century was the centre of the Parisian tailors, just as the Rue de la Paix is to-day. They were also called the *grands courriers de la mode*, under which title they were invoiced as having arrived at Dover in 1764. These fashion dolls were made life-size in order that the clothes with

FIG. 137. ENGLISH DOLL OF THE REIGN OF QUEEN ANNE
Victoria and Albert Museum

which they were dressed might be immediately worn. "The *chic* imparted to fashion by French hands," writes Mercier in his *Tableau de Paris*, "is imitated by all nations, who obediently submit to the taste of the Rue Saint-Honoré." Mercier, a good journalist, once took a stranger who doubted the existence of the fashion doll to Rose Bertin in order to convince him that it was a reality. Rose Bertin was the dressmaker of the elegant world; she worked for the Queen, and neither she nor the other Court dressmaker, Mme Éloffe, neglected the dressed-up mannequins. In 1777 Bertin clothed for Prince Rohan-Guéménée a large, beautifully coiffeured doll in a ball dress of white-and-rose silk over the hoop petticoat. It was to have cost 300 francs, but that sum was never received by the dressmaker, for the Rohan family went bankrupt in millions. Mme Éloffe supplied the Comtesse Bombelles on August 18, 1788, with a life-size mannequin in Court dress for 409 francs, 12 centimes. Marie-Antoinette took pleasure, through the good offices of the furniture-designer

FIG. 138. ENGLISH DOLL'S SHOP, ABOUT 1850
Presented to the Bethnal Green Museum, London, by Miss Lester Garland
By permission of the Victoria and Albert Museum

David Röntgen, of Neuwied, in sending to her mother and sisters dolls dressed in the latest Parisian styles. Risbeck too, who visited Vienna in the last decade of the century, mentions them: "French fashion rules here despotically. Periodically mannequins are sent here [Vienna] from Paris and serve the ladies as models for their dresses and head-gear."

Not only dressmakers, but hairdressers made use of dolls. Thus on one occasion Mme de Sévigné promised her daughter a doll coiffeured according to the latest mode, while Melchior Grimm described in his well-known correspondence how the hairdresser Legros, who was the most popular Parisian 'hair-artist' in the time of the Pompadour, had many enemies, and how these had

DOLLS AND PUPPETS

been silenced by the exhibition of thirty coiffeured dolls at the annual fair of Saint-Ovide in 1763. These beautiful dolls, to which was entrusted so important a cultural mission in the spreading of French fashion, have even found poets to sing their praises. Algarotti, in his Italian epistle to Phyllis, celebrated in song the

FIG. 139. ENGLISH WAX DOLL, ABOUT 1780
Presented to the Victoria and Albert Museum by Miss Ethel Diton

FIG. 140. ENGLISH DOLL WITH WAX HEAD, ABOUT 1800
Presented to the Bethnal Green Museum, London, by Mrs Greg

By permission of the Victoria and Albert Museum

charm of the French mannequin, and Delille, a fashionable French poet of the day, in 1786 praised Rose Bertin's dolls:

Et jusqu'au fond du Nord portant nos goûts divers,
Le mannequin despote asservit l'univers.

The French example did not remain unimitated. *The Gentleman's Magazine* contained a note in 1751 to the effect that several mannequins with different styles of dress had been made in St James's Street in order to give the Tsarina (Elizabeth) an idea of the manner of dressing which at the moment was in fashion among the English ladies. Catharine II designed articles of an absolutely unique cut for the young grand dukes, and in order to show King Gustavus III of Sweden how she clothed her grandchildren she got dolls made and dressed according to her directions. In the end the Parisian fashion mannequins succeeded in reaching North America. In *The New England*

FIG. 141. GIRL WITH DOLL
Sir Joshua Reynolds. About 1785

Weekly Journal of July 2, 1733, appeared the following advertisement:

At Mrs Hannah Teatt's, dressmaker at the top of Summer Street, Boston, is to be seen a mannequin, in the latest fashion, with articles of dress, night dresses, and everything appertaining to women's attire. It has been brought from London by Captain White. Ladies who choose to see it may come or send for it. It is always ready to serve you. If you come, it will cost you two shillings, but if you send for it, seven shillings.

In similar manner, only in a less flowery style, two dressmakers of Irish nationality in New York advertised in 1757 to the effect that the latest mannequins had arrived from London. In 1796 a certain Sally MacKean wrote to her friend Dolly Madison, "Yesterday I went to see a mannequin which has just come from England to give us an idea of the latest fashions."

FIG. 142. ENGLISH DOLL, ABOUT 1860
Presented to the Bethnal Green Museum, London, by Mrs Greg
By permission of the Victoria and Albert Museum

It need not, however, be concealed that very soon the suspicion developed abroad that the Parisian tailors and dressmakers were making use of these mannequins merely for the purpose of getting rid of their old stock. Horace Walpole wrote from Paris on September 22, 1765, to George Montague: "The French have become very plain in their dress. We English still pray to their old idols." Even Prince Henry of Prussia, who in 1769 asked Darget to get him some cloth from Paris, thought it necessary to add a warning that he did not wish for such as had been made for German princes and barons, but the sort which the Prince

FIG. 143. MALE AND FEMALE PEDLARS (PORTSMOUTH), ABOUT 1810
Presented to the Bethnal Green Museum, London, by Mrs Greg
By permission of the Victoria and Albert Museum

FIG. 144. FLAT PAINTED FIGURES
Lady with fan, man smoking, man with a muff. Eighteenth century
Bayerisches National-Museum, Munich

de Conti and the Marshals Contades and d'Estrées were then wearing. The wars of the French Republic and of Napolecn I put an end to the free passage of the mannequins, nor were these so necessary now that the fashion journals provided a complete substitute. Their use, however, has not wholly ceased. French fashion mannequins cost eighty francs before the War, and many

FIG. 145. ENGLISH MOVABLE FASHION DOLLS, ABOUT 1830

such figures, about a metre high, along with complete *trousseaux*, were supplied for the harems of some Oriental grandees.

England was responsible for the invention of one particular kind of figure used for the purpose of displaying new fashions in dress. Up to comparatively recent times the English tradition in regard to the toy doll is remarkably meagre; indeed, it seems that originally English dolls had no special name allotted to them. They were simply called 'little ladies' or 'babies,' and it is only in the eighteenth century that the expression 'doll' begins to be used. The English themselves are in doubt con-

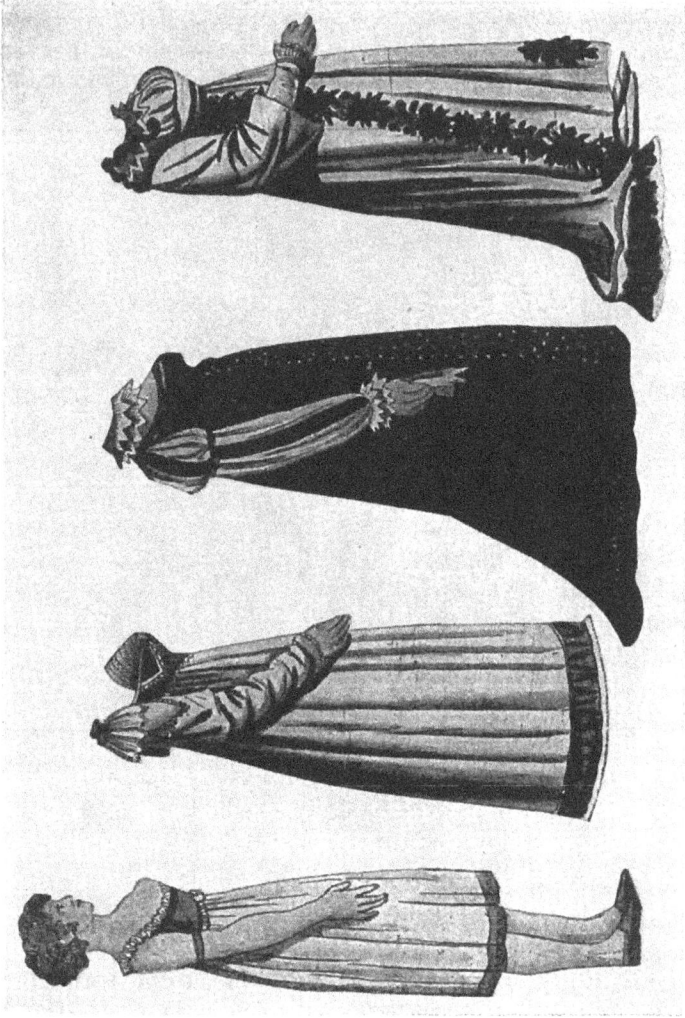

cerning the etymology of this word. Some consider that the term 'doll' is connected with the diminutive of endearment

FIG. 146. ENGLISH WAX DOLL, MIDDLE OF THE NINETEENTH CENTURY
Presented to the Victoria and Albert Museum by Frank Green

'Dolly' (for Dorothy); others think it is a derivative from 'idol'; still others turn to the Norse *daul*, which signifies a female domestic servant. Even though we know almost nothing about the older periods, it must be presumed that the little English girls

DOLLS AND PUPPETS

had their dolls. The portrait painted about the year 1600 of Lady Arabella Stuart as a child shows her with her doll dressed exactly like a grown-up woman, just as were the German and

FIG. 147. TRICK DOLLS OF PRESSED AND CUT-OUT CARDBOARD
(METAMORPHOSES)
Germanisches National-Museum, Nürnberg

French toy dolls of that time. Only toward the end of the eighteenth century did England enrich the doll world with new inventions. Silhouettes cut out of paper had been known for a long time in Germany; in the Germanische National-Museum, in Nürnberg, is a picture-sheet of the seventeenth century with fashion-plates intended to be cut out; but the English made out of this something entirely new. They invented the one-sided figures to be cut out of paper, for which many different garments were provided, the costumes thus being rendered changeable. These paper figures, 8 in. high and supplied with six sets of clothes, were put on the market in 1790 by English firms. In the *Journal des Luxus und der Moden* of 1791 they are called attention to, and Bertuch, who was always on the look-out for novelties, at once proceeded to imitate them. Such a figure, with its wardrobe of six changes, cost then three shillings. The French adopted this invention as a means of cheap advertisement for their fashions; Gavarni, for example, lithographed a whole series of such fashion-plates intended to be cut out.

FIG. 148. MANNEQUIN

www.ingramcontent.com/pod-product-compliance
Lightning Source LLC
Chambersburg PA
CBHW031142270326
41931CB00007B/666